Understanding Charts and Graphs

C H R I S T I N E   T A Y L O R - B U T L E R

Children's Press®
An Imprint of Scholastic Inc.
New York Toronto London Auckland Sydney
Mexico City New Delhi Hong Kong
Danbury, Connecticut

Content Consultant

Nabil Al-Najjar, PhD
Professor and Chair, Managerial Economics & Decision Making Sciences Department
Kellogg School of Management
Northwestern University
Evanston, Illinois

Library of Congress Cataloging-in-Publication Data

Taylor-Butler, Christine.
  Understanding charts and graphs/by Christine Taylor-Butler.
      p. cm.—(A true book)
  Includes bibliographical references and index.
    ISBN 978-0-531-26009-8 (lib. bdg.) — ISBN 978-0-531-26240-5 (pbk.)
  1. Mathematical statistics—Juvenile literature. 2. Mathematics—Graphic methods—Juvenile literature. I. Title.
  QA273.16.T39 2012
  001.4'226—dc23   2012002643

All rights reserved. Published in 2013 by Children's Press, an imprint of Scholastic Inc.
Printed in China 62
SCHOLASTIC, CHILDREN'S PRESS, A TRUE BOOK™, and associated logos are trademarks and/or registered trademarks of Scholastic Inc.
1 2 3 4 5 6 7 8 9 10 R 22 21 20 19 18 17 16 15 14 13

Front cover: Pie chart, bar graph, and line graph
Back cover: Weather map

Find the Truth!

Everything you are about to read is true *except* for one of the sentences on this page.

Which one is **TRUE**?

T or F Spreadsheets were tablecloths used by tax collectors to count the king's money.

T or F The oldest known Mayan calendar dates as far as 7012 CE.

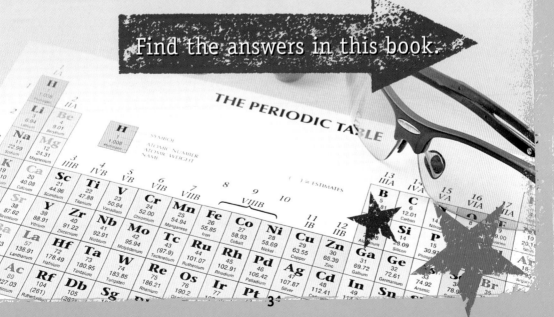

Find the answers in this book.

3

Contents

1 Don't Say It-Show It!

What were some of the earliest
graphic organizers? 7

2 Put It on the Table

Which professions commonly use tables? 15

THE BIG TRUTH!

March Madness

How does the NCAA chart its basketball
championship games? 22

3 Graph It Out!

What are some ways to compare
two sets of data? 25

6%

13%

75%

4 Charts

Charts and graphs help organize complex infromation.

How can words, numbers, and pictures help organize
information? **35**

True Statistics **44**

Resources **45**

Important Words **46**

Index **47**

About the Author **48**

Ancient Mayans carved calendars in stone and painted them on walls.

CHAPTER 1

Don't Say It–Show It!

Imagine visiting a restaurant. The waitress describes 100 meals the chef can prepare. Can you remember all the choices? How do you choose what to eat?

You ask for a menu. The menu is divided into groups: appetizers, soups and salads, main courses, desserts, and drinks. Does that make it easier to choose? It probably does. A menu is one example of a chart.

 The largest restaurant in the world has 6,014 seats.

7

Graphic Organizers

People come across charts, tables, and graphs in everyday life. Calendars keep track of important dates. Doctors record your health information on a medical chart. Engineers use flowcharts and graphs to plan large projects. Teachers use charts to show student progress and to record grades. Artists and writers use charts to brainstorm new ideas. Musicians use charts when they read sheet music. Another name for a chart, table, or graph is *graphic organizer*.

Doctors and nurses use graphic organizers to help them keep track of important patient information.

Calendars helped the Maya keep track of religious celebrations and other events.

The earliest graphic organizers date back thousands of years. Stone carvings of game boards appear in ancient Egyptian temples. The Mayan civilization created calendars that counted as far out as the year 7012 CE. Mathematicians and philosophers have used charts to teach logic problems for thousands of years.

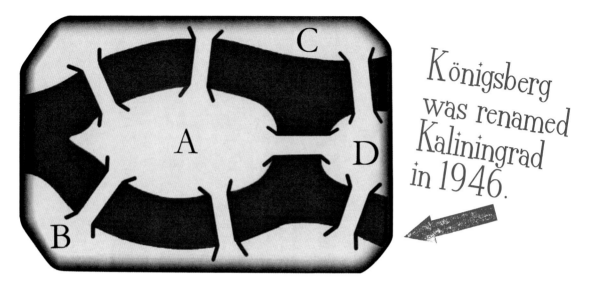

Königsberg was renamed Kaliningrad in 1946.

Leonhard Euler's map of bridge paths was one of the first modern graphs.

Inventive Organizers

In 1736, Swiss mathematician Leonhard Euler came up with the first modern ideas about graphs. He looked at the seven bridges that crossed a river running through the city of Königsberg, in present-day Russia. He wanted to prove that it was impossible to find a single path around the city that would cross each bridge only once. He used a series of **nodes** and lines to show the possible paths. An even number of bridges was needed to solve the problem.

In the 1780s, Scottish engineer William Playfair drew the first line and bar graphs. He used them to track goods being shipped between England and other countries. He thought a picture would be easier to understand than the columns of numbers normally used for this task. Playfair later drew circles with shaded sections to compare different areas of land. These circle graphs became the first known pie charts.

Pie charts are used often in modern business presentations.

11

The first digital table software, VisiCalc, was introduced in 1979. It became popular because it could sort data and perform math calculations quickly. Today, businesses use these tables, or spreadsheets, to look for trends and patterns. Scientists use them to make comparisons and draw conclusions from complicated data.

Spreadsheets help organize large amounts of data, making the information easier to analyze.

Spreadsheet programs are often used to turn data into other graphic organizers.

Spreadsheets can create more than one type of chart from the same data. The table of numbers is turned into pie charts, line graphs, and other graphic organizers so the data can be analyzed more easily. Presentation software such as PowerPoint makes it easy to share the information with large groups.

Departures

Departing To	Flight	Time	Status	Terminal	Gate
Portland, OR	6464				
Providence	3075	10:00A	On Time	C	127
Quebec City	2241	12:30P	On Time	C	111a
Quebec City	2835	9:15A	Now 10:35 AM	C	108b
Raleigh/Durham	5689	12:40P	On Time	C	106a
Raleigh/Durham	5161	11:05A	On Time	C	106a
Richmond	7392	1:35P	On Time	C	108b
Rochester, NY	9490	12:30P	On Time	C	107b
Rochester, NY	5542	4:55P	DEPARTED	C	103a
San Diego	2443	1:05P	On Time	C	113a
San Francisco	248	1:10P	On Time	C	94
San Juan	6572	11:15A	On Time	C	72
Seattle/Tacoma	3019	12:50P	On Time	C	128
		2:00P	On Time	C	84

Wednesday November 21 2007 9:24 AM

Departures

Continental Airlines

Departing To	Flight	Time	Status	Terminal	Gate
mford-Rail	9411	10:18A	On Time	-	RAIL
mford-Rail	9422	12:19P	On Time	-	RAIL
use	3392	1:00P	On Time	C	114a
a	6610	10:25A	On Time	C	137
Narita	6618	11:30A	On Time	C	70
	6009	11:10A	On Time	C	75
	2215	10:10A	On Time	C	101a
lles	5325	11:15A	On Time	C	113b
gan Natl	2175	1:00P	On Time	A	27
gan Natl	2140	11:00A	On Time	A	25
Beach	6209	1:00P	On Time	A	25
Beach	6040	10:35A	On Time	C	84
	6290	1:25P	On Time	C	136

Wednesday November 21 2007 9:24 AM

CHAPTER 2

Put It on the Table

Suppose you are visiting an airport. You want to know when your flight will leave. A monitor shows each airline, with each plane's flight number, time of departure, and gate where passengers will board. The chart is arranged as a table. The flight schedules are arranged in rows and columns, and are sorted by city or departure time. Tables make it easy to find information quickly.

There are an estimated 28,000 airline flights each day in the United States.

Just the Facts

You probably use tables almost every day. A book's list of contents, an index, and even the ingredients on a box of cereal are examples of tables. You may also see tables in the classroom. A periodic table in your science class is one example. Students use addition, subtraction, multiplication, and division tables to learn math facts.

The periodic table is a necessary tool for learning about chemistry.

16

Try It!

You can make your own math fact sheet. Here's how:
1. On a sheet of notebook paper, copy the chart below.
2. Multiply the numbers of the column (1) to the row (1) that **intersect** at the first blank box at the top left corner of the chart. Place the answer in the box, as shown below.
3. Do the same for the other boxes, adding the numbers for the column and row that intersect at each box. Try timing yourself with a stopwatch or a clock with a second hand. How fast can you fill in the spaces?

Math fact sheets are good tools to use to practice for a test.

	1	2	3	4	5	6	7	8	9	10
1	1									
2										
3										
4										
5										
6										
7										
8										
9										
10										

Spreadsheets

Accountants and businesses use spreadsheets to keep track of money. Computer programs such as Excel can automatically add and subtract **credits** and **debits** when they are entered into the spreadsheet. This provides an up-to-date account balance, or total. Scientists who keep track of the results of experiments can use the program to calculate percentages and other information. The programs can also reorganize data according to date, size, or other guides.

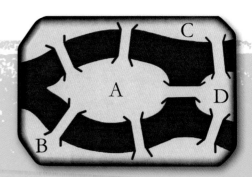

A Timeline of Charts and Graphs

1100s

Counting tables are used by King Henry II's treasurer to count taxes.

1736

Leonhard Euler writes the first paper describing graph theory.

Spreadsheets do not only deal in numbers. Words and phrases can be entered to organize people or events. Businesses and individuals can use spreadsheets to outline a schedule or track the progress of a project. Contact lists that include home addresses, phone numbers, and email addresses can be kept updated and alphabetized. People even use spreadsheet software to create to-do lists and checklists.

+45%	+58%
+25%	+46%
+20%	+44%
+29%	+10%
-15%	+15%
+4%	+24%
+34%	

1801
William Playfair publishes *The Commercial and Political Atlas* and *The Statistical Breviary*, containing the first bar, line, and pie charts.

1858
French engineer Joseph Minard begins using pie charts in his work.

1979
Dan Bricklin and Bob Frankston invent VisiCalc, the first computer spreadsheet.

Personal Planners

A personal planner contains a calendar and a to-do list. Businesspeople use personal planners to help them remember the details of their schedules. Students throughout the world use planners to keep track of appointments, class times, homework assignments, and test dates.

The first 365-day calendar was introduced in ancient Egypt.

Planners are a great way to keep track of upcoming events.

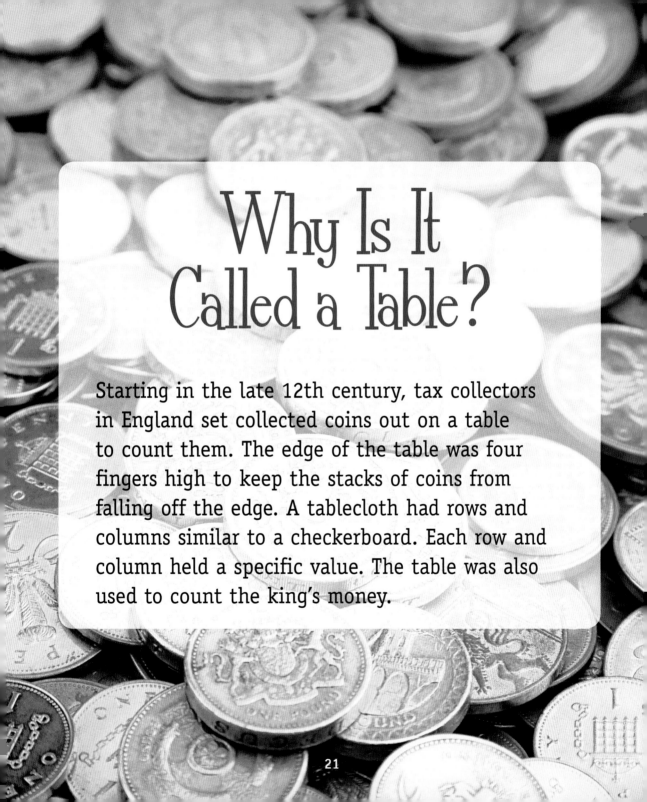

Why Is It Called a Table?

Starting in the late 12th century, tax collectors in England set collected coins out on a table to count them. The edge of the table was four fingers high to keep the stacks of coins from falling off the edge. A tablecloth had rows and columns similar to a checkerboard. Each row and column held a specific value. The table was also used to count the king's money.

March Madness

Sports brackets keep track of winners and losers in a competition or event. The National Collegiate Athletic Association (NCAA) March Madness championship is one example. The tournament hosts 68 teams in the men's division and 64 teams in the women's division. The teams compete from March until April.

1 Teams are grouped into four regions. The regional teams are then paired for matches.

2 The winner of each match advances to the next round, in which they compete against the winner of another match.

3 The winners continue to advance on the chart until only one team remains.

4 The final winning team is declared the champion.

2012 NCAA March Madness Results

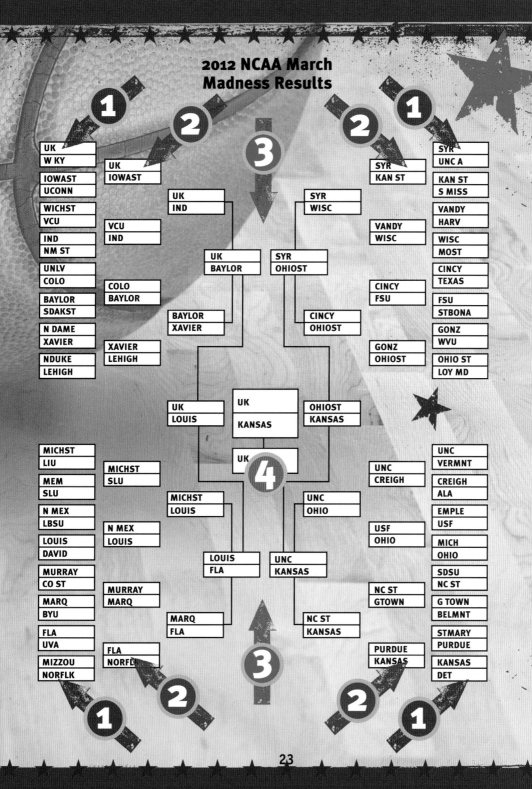

Dow Jones Industrial Average
(1920 - 1940 Daily)

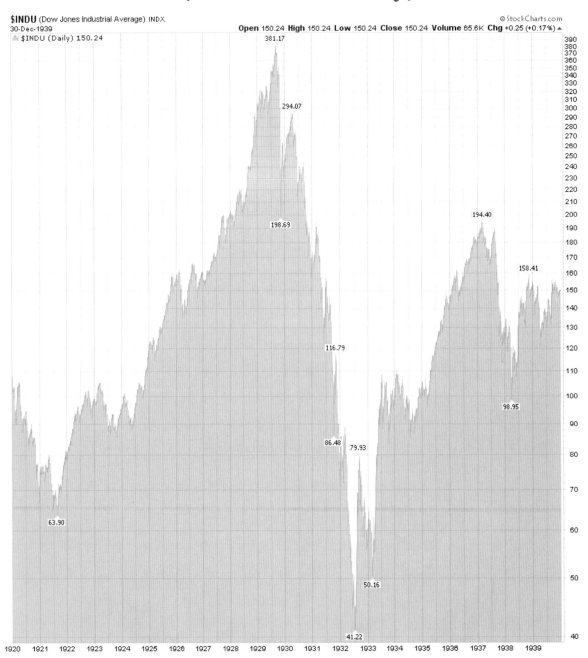

CHAPTER 3

Graph It Out!

Graphs measure data that change over time. The data are called **variables**. Some graphs use a grid made from two main lines. Each line is called an **axis**. The horizontal line is called the x-axis. The vertical line is called the y-axis. Graphs can compare more than one variable at once.

This line graphs shows that between 1920 and 1929, stock prices increased by 400 percent.

Line Graph

Entering data on a graph is called **plotting**. The location on the graph is called a **coordinate** point. Coordinate points are connected by a line.

A graph includes many parts:

Title: This tells a reader what the graph is about.

Legend: When a graph has more than one line, this tells what each line represents.

X-Axis: This shows the time period in units that the data covers.

Y-Axis: This shows the units used for measuring the data.

Data: This is the information being measured.

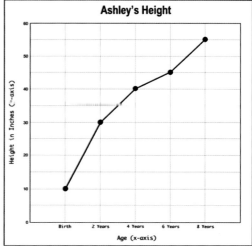

Line graphs are good for keeping track of how something increases or decreases over time.

Try It!

Make a graph of your local weather over the period of a week.

1. On a sheet of notebook paper, copy the graph below. The degrees listed on your y-axis may need to start at a higher or lower temperature, depending on how warm it is outside. It does not need to start at zero. List temperatures by tens.

2. Check the temperature at the same time each day. You can either use a thermometer or check the temperature on a weather Web site.

3. Record your data at the point where the appropriate day and the temperature intersect on the graph.

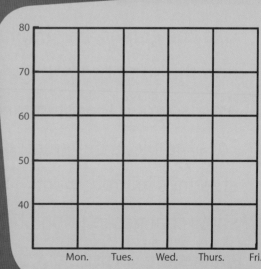

World Population by Continent

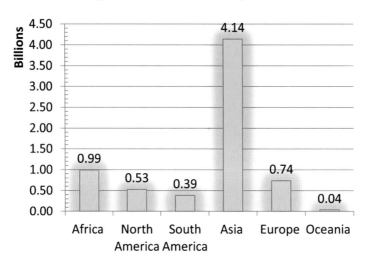

Bar graphs make it easy for people to see how different measurements compare to one another.

Bar Graphs

Like line graphs, bar graphs are useful for showing how the size of something changes over time. They are also good for comparing different groups of data. For example, a bar graph might be used to show a student's improvement in test scores. Or it could show changes in population. The most common bar graphs are vertical, but some are horizontal.

Try It!

Create a bar graph to compare the populations of Alaska, New Jersey, and Iowa. Here's how:

1. On a sheet of notebook paper, copy the graph below.
2. Visit the U.S. Census Bureau Population Finder Web site at *www.census.gov/popfinder/*. Find Alaska in the drop-down menu, and click "Display."
3. In Alaska's section, draw a bar that reaches the appropriate total population on the y-axis. Round the number to the nearest million.
4. Repeat steps 2 and 3 for the other two states.
5. Give your graph a title. How does each state's population compare to other states?

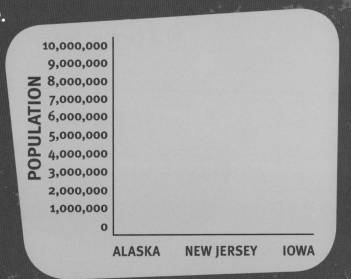

Pie Charts

Unlike line and bar graphs, circle graphs show percentages. Circle graphs are also known as pie charts because each section looks like a slice of pie. Each slice represents a fraction or percentage of the whole. The U.S. Census Bureau sometimes uses pie charts to show how many men versus women live in the United States. A pie chart can also show how the population is divided according to age or ethnic group.

Census statistics are often represented using circle graphs.

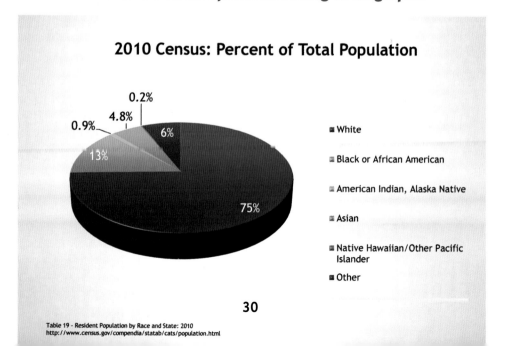

2010 Census: Percent of Total Population

0.2%
4.8%
0.9%
6%
13%
75%

- White
- Black or African American
- American Indian, Alaska Native
- Asian
- Native Hawaiian/Other Pacific Islander
- Other

30

Table 19 - Resident Population by Race and State: 2010
http://www.census.gov/compendia/statab/cats/population.html

Try It!

Create a pie chart showing your classmates' favorite hobbies. You might want to ask your teacher if you can do this as a class project. Follow these directions:

1. On a sheet of notebook paper, list three options, such as reading, video games, and sports.
2. Take a **poll**, asking each of your classmates to choose their favorite of the options.
3. For each hobby, divide the number of students who chose it by the total number of students. Multiply this number by 100 to find the percentage.
4. Draw a circle on a piece of notebook paper. Divide this chart into sections based on the percentage who chose each hobby.
5. Draw a legend to show what each section of the chart represents.

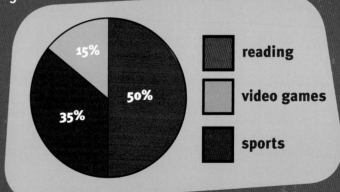

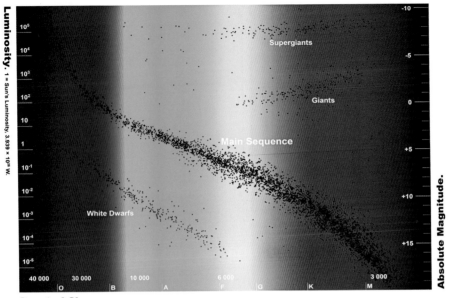

Luminosity. 1 = Sun's Luminosity, 3.939 × 10²⁶ W.

Absolute Magnitude.

Spectral Class And Surface Temperature (K°).

Scientists use this scatter plot graph, called the Hertzprung-Russell Diagram, to study how stars' colors relate to how brightly they shine.

Scatter Plot Graphs

Data does not always follow a logical pattern. Scatter plots are useful for comparing more than one type of variable. Scientists use this graph to determine if there is a relationship between the data. If the data are close together, they are related. If the data are scattered all over the place, they are not. A line is sometimes drawn between the points to find an **average**.

Try It!

Create a scatter plot of your friends' and family members' birthdays. Try to use at least 10 people. Follow these directions:

1. Copy the chart below on a sheet of notebook paper.
2. Place a dot at the intersection of the month and date of each friend's birthday. What are the most common months? What are the most common days? Is there any relationship between months and days? Sometimes there is not.

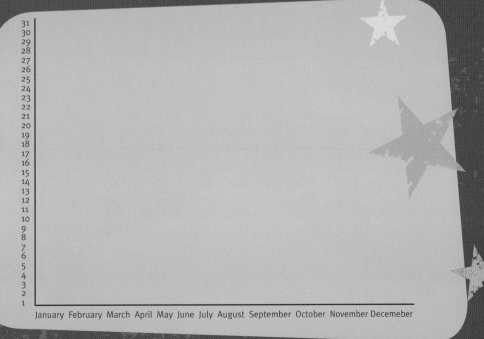

CHAPTER 4

Charts

Charts are a good way of showing information with words, pictures, or numbers. Charts in a classroom might show math facts, grammar rules, or even student progress. They can be used to show relationships between people, places, or things. Scientists, engineers, and businesses use charts to show data that does not change for a long time.

 Sailors use charts to help navigate through large bodies of water.

Flowcharts

Flowcharts show how things or events are organized. They list each task in order. This is called a **sequence**. Engineers use flowcharts to list the sequence of steps needed to build something. Businesses use flowcharts to show the sequence of actions needed to make a decision. Flowcharts get their name because each task on a chart flows into another.

Construction workers use flowcharts to make sure they complete each part of a project in the right order.

Try It!

Create your own flowchart for an activity, such as baking cookies. Here's how:

1. Write down the steps that must take place to do the activity. What steps come first? Which come next? Some steps in a sequence do not depend on one another. Others can only work in a certain order. For example, you can gather ingredients before you turn on the oven. But you must turn on the oven before you are done mixing the ingredients so it will be hot enough when the dough is ready to bake.

2. Copy the steps into a flowchart, numbering each step in sequence.

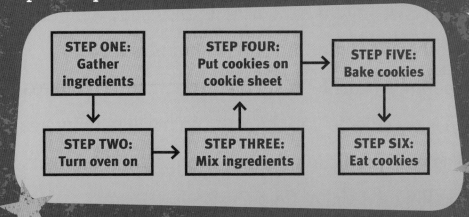

STEP ONE: Gather ingredients

STEP TWO: Turn oven on

STEP THREE: Mix ingredients

STEP FOUR: Put cookies on cookie sheet

STEP FIVE: Bake cookies

STEP SIX: Eat cookies

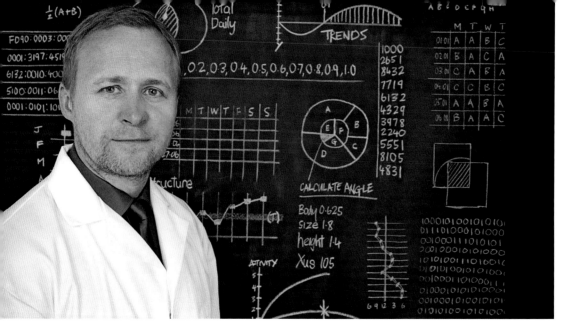

Scientists must often analyze very complicated data in order to predict the outcome of experiments.

Prediction Charts

Scientists conduct experiments to find the answer to a question. They use their knowledge to guess what the answer might be. This guess is called a prediction. Another word for prediction is **hypothesis**. Try creating a chart for a simple experiment: a coin toss. On what side do you think the coin will fall? Try again. Was your prediction right or wrong? What happens if you flip the coin 20 times?

Try It!

Prediction charts are useful for other projects, too. When you read a book, do you try to predict what will happen next? A prediction chart is a good way of making notes and reviewing what you've read. Here's how you can use one:

1. Copy the chart below on a piece of notebook paper.
2. Write down predictions about a book you are reading.
3. When you've finished the book, compare your predictions to the book's real ending. Were you correct?

My Prediction	Why I Made This Prediciton	Was My Prediction Correct?	
		Yes	No

Character-Traits Charts

Authors often make charts to keep track of character-traits. A trait describes the way a character looks, talks, or feels. A character-traits chart helps an author remember which character has brown eyes and which has green ones. The chart might show how a character reacts to a problem. Is the character timid or brave when danger is near?

NAME _____ DATE _____

Character-Traits Chart

Character's Name	Describe the Character	Analyze the Character and His or Her Actions

The most characters given individual voices in an audio book is 224, in George R. R. Martin's A Game of Thrones.

A character-traits chart can be very helpful if you are writing a story.

The Family Tree

Genealogy is the study of families and their ancestors. One way of recording this information is to create a chart. The chart shows how each member of a family is related to another. The diagram is called a family tree because of its shape. Each part of a family branches out to connect to new family members.

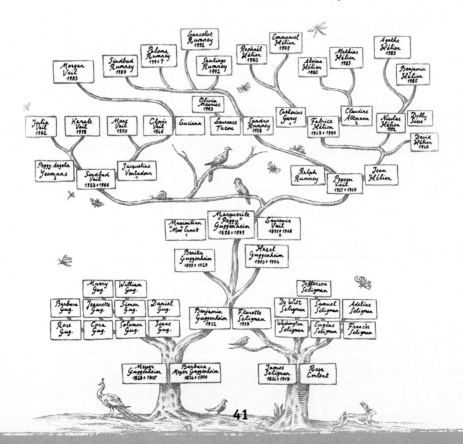

Note-Taking Organizer

MY NOTES

Main points from my notes
1. _____
_____
2. _____
_____
3. _____
_____

Two questions I still have
1. _____
_____
2. _____
_____

Strategies that I will use to answer my questions.
_____
_____
_____
_____
_____

Organized notes are much easier to use than sloppy ones.

Note-Taking Charts

Charts can be used to make notes about questions you have. They can be used when taking notes in class, while planning a project, or when brainstorming an idea. Try using this note-taking chart when studying for an assignment. What are the subject's main points? What questions do you have? Where can you go to find the answers?

Organization for Any Occasion

There are countless varieties of charts and graphs from which to choose. If you cannot find the perfect one for your task, you can adapt one to fit. Whether you are comparing data, tracking variables, taking a poll, or just trying to decide what food to order, a graphic organizer can help you out. ★

The right chart can make any task simpler.

True Statistics

Number of people in the world: 7 billion, as of 2012

Number of people in the United States: 313 million, as of 2012

Number of U.S. accountants and auditors in 2008: 1.3 million

Average U.S. family size in 2010: 2.59

Total number of passengers flying through the United States in 2010: 786.7 million

Number of available rows in an Excel spreadsheet as of 2012: More than 1 million

Year the periodic table was first developed: 1869, by Dmitry Mendeleyev

Age of the oldest known lunar calendar: 15,000 years

Did you find the truth?

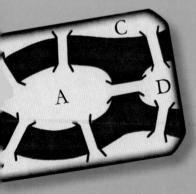

F Spreadsheets were tablecloths used by tax collectors to count the king's money.

T The oldest known Mayan calendar shows dates as far as 7012 CE.

Resources

Books

Dowdy, Penny. *Graphing*. New York: Crabtree Publishing, 2008.

Piddock, Claire. *Line, Bar, and Circle Graphs*. New York: Crabtree Publishing, 2010.

Priestley, Michael. *Charts, Tables, and Graphs*. New York: Teaching Resources, 2005.

Taylor-Butler, Christine. *Understanding Diagrams*. New York: Children's Press, 2013.

Visit this Scholastic Web site for more information on understanding charts and graphs:
www.factsfornow.scholastic.com
★ Enter the keywords **Charts and Graphs**

Important Words

average (AV-ur-ij) — a number that you get by adding a group of numbers together and then dividing the sum by the number of figures you have added

axis (AK-sis) — a line at the side or the bottom of a graph

coordinate (koh-OR-duh-nit) — describing all or part of a set of numbers used to show the position of a point on a line, graph, or map

credits (KRED-its) — records of money that is added to an account

debits (DEB-its) — records of money that is taken out of an account

hypothesis (hye-PAH-thi-sis) — an idea that could explain how something works but that has to be tested through experiments to be proven

intersect (in-tur-SEKT) — to meet or cross something

nodes (NOHDZ) — points at which lines or pathways intersect

plotting (PLAHT-ing) — marking out something based on calculations

poll (POHL) — a survey of people's opinions or beliefs

sequence (SEE-kwuhns) — a series or collection of things that follow each other in a particular order

variables (VAIR-ee-uh-buhlz) — data that change over time

Index

Page numbers in **bold** indicate illustrations

averages, 32
axis lines, 25, 26, 27, 29

bar graphs, 11, 13, 19, **28**, **29**
Bricklin, Dan, 19

calendars, 8, **9**, 20
character-traits charts, **40**
circle graphs. *See* pie charts.
coordinate points, 26
counting tables, **18**, **21**
credits, 18, 19

data, 12, 13, 25, 26, 28, 32, 35, **38**
debits, 18, 19

Euler, Leonhard, **10**, 18
Excel software, 18

family trees, **41**
flight schedules, **14**, 15
flowcharts, 8, **36**, 37
Frankston, Bob, 19

genealogy, 41

Hertzprung-Russell Diagram, **32**
hypotheses, **38**

Königsberg map, **10**

legends, 26, 31
line graphs, 11, 13, 19, **24**, 25, **26**, 27

March Madness, 22–23
mathematics, 9, 10, 12, 16, **17**
Mayan civilization, **9**

medical charts, **8**
menus, **6**, 7
Minard, Joseph, 19

navigation charts, **34**, 35
note-taking charts, **42**

percentages, 30, 31
periodic table, **16**
personal planners, **20**
pic charts, **11**, 13, 19, **30**, 31
Playfair, William, 11, 19
plotting, 26
PowerPoint software, 13
prediction charts, 38, **39**
programs. *See* software.

scatter plot graphs, **32**, **33**
sequence, 36, 37
software, 12, 18
sports brackets, 22, **23**
spreadsheets, 12, **13**, **18**, **19**
stocks, **24**, 25

tax collectors, **12**, **21**
timeline, **12–13**
titles, 26

U.S. Census Bureau, 29, 30

variables, 25, 32
VisiCalc software, 12, 19

x-axis lines, 25, 26, 29

y-axis lines, 25, 26, 27, 29

About the Author

Christine Taylor-Butler is the author of more than 60 books for children, including the True Book series on American History/Government, Health and the Human Body, and Science Experiments. A graduate of the Massachusetts Institute of Technology, Christine holds degrees in both civil engineering and art and design. She currently lives in Kansas City, Missouri.